I0802008

Praise for Cinematic Taxi

Corrado Paina's *Cinematic Taxi* is a twenty-first century response to Dennis Lee's *Civil Elegies*, a call-out to civic identity based not on local expressions of nationalism but an interrogation of culture itself.

A scathing critique of multiculturalism, it alternately scolds, seduces and shocks its interlocutor into sensing the emptiness of appeals to heritage and hyphenation in which "italoportojapokrainian" citizens –"the ethnics"– are reduced to the odours of their food and sweat.

Travelling from the neoclassical garages of Woodbridge – "the Petawawa of the rich" – to damp streetcars, refuse-strewn taxis and anxious immigrants' line-ups at Honest Ed's, this collection culminates in a transliteration in which broken English melded with idiomatic Italian – a patois underscoring the impossibility of communicating across cultures too besotted with the material accomplishments of their lives to realize they've become confined to their "maximum security bekiardas."

—**Amy Lavender Harris**, author of *Imagining Toronto*

Corrado Paina brings his unique perspective to the great experiment that is Toronto. Generations of immigrants have made this city home, and make this city today one of the world's most diverse. Although largely harmonious, Toronto is still home to inequities and inequalities, all of which are explored in this distinctive work

—**David Miller,** former Mayor of Toronto

What is most exciting is that these poems challenge some of the assumptions of our own Canadian 'Babylon.' It's as if the Lombards, the original barbarians, are here to remind us that we cannot remain complacent, that we somehow need to make sense of the cacophony we are constructing lest it slip into a chaos that would dismantle everything we have built.

For the reader the reward is powerful and the translation of the poems into a Milanese dialect, yet shaded by 'Italiese' (the combination of Italian and English unique to Italian-Canadians) is a reminder of the power of this new Babylon, which is generating a multiplicity of realities that fragment the narratives of our industrial society and its co-requisite nation state. Paina is a reluctant voyager into this new world, but such a prescient observer.

—**Luigi Ferrara**, Dean of the Centre for Arts & Design,
George Brown College

Paina's book not only stands as a monument to the immigrant experience but also, and perhaps more importantly, as a testament to 'otherness' in every conceivable instance, including that of the creative artist whose estrangement from the world allows for a glimpse into human existence.

—**Donato Santeramo**, Head, Department of Languages, Literatures and Cultures, Queen's University.

...Paina's other theme, is multiculturalism, a topic about which he has decidedly mixed feelings. "Saving traditions" he has argued, "is worse than killing a culture...." Except that, as Paina understands well, the results are new mongrel traditions with which Toronto abounds. Situating himself in the centre of the cultural tumult, immersed in the unfolding spectacle that is the big city, he neither completely decries nor celebrates. It is enough to bear witness, to behold the city as it is regardless of whether we know or not.

—**Christopher Hume,** *Toronto Star*

In a captivating journey of intersected paths, Corrado Paina's *Cinematic Taxi* appropriates urban physical spaces and transforms them into vibrant and forceful metaphors of our current multi-ethnic, multilingual and multicultural landscapes. Just as the labyrinth of shelves and aisles of Honest Ed's, with its hodgepodge of disparate and varied wares became the undisputed witness to Toronto's innumerable immigrant histories, Paina witnesses, but above all engages, questions, observes and reveals, what has become and is becoming of those histories. He masterfully crosses borders between physical and emotional spaces. Borders and histories are repeatedly forgotten, recreated and approximated as he challenges the reader to reflect upon and take part in an ongoing attempt to define meaning and to shape or re-shape identity. Language and languages become a vehicle of fragmented identity. The hybrid knows no boundaries. In a polyphony of sounds and multiplicity of voices the multicultural and translingual self is continuously re-written and re-defined as we shape our perceptions of the world and our own self-perceptions. He skilfully invites us, in other words, to share in his writing of his/our history.

—**Bruno Magliocchetti**, University of Toronto

CINEMATIC TAXI

CINEMATIC TAXI

Corrado Paina

Mansfield Press

Printed in Canada

Library and Archives Canada Cataloguing in Publication

Paina, Corrado, 1954-, author
Cinematic taxi / Corrado Paina.

Revisits poems from his book Hoarse legend and translates into his own language.
Poems.
ISBN 978-1-77126-065-7 (pbk.)

I. Title.

PS8581.A4843C55 2014 C811'.6 C2014-907532-4

Design: Denis De Klerck
Cover Photo: Shutterstock

The publication of *Cinematic Taxi* has been generously supported by the Canada Council for the Arts and the Ontario Arts Council.

Canada Council for the Arts Conseil des Arts du Canada

ONTARIO ARTS COUNCIL
CONSEIL DES ARTS DE L'ONTARIO

Mansfield Press Inc.
25 Mansfield Avenue, Toronto, Ontario, Canada M6J 2A9
Publisher: Denis De Klerck
www.mansfieldpress.net

Canary Wharf

another day unfolds
to repeat the language
of an advanced lineage

dominant races with confused grimaces
in the shadows of Charlottetown
in the variety stores of Meech Lake

the damp streetcars don't provide shelter
or work   on a journey backwards
zealous porters escort to Limbo

we leave theatres under the bridges
we leave cubans in exile that
scatter notes like croissants

look

waning is the drunkenness of the aboriginals
now reclined, crucified from dizziness

the stench of chamber pots floods Queen Street
in that corner where the streetcar observes silently

eloquent rows of immigrants' children
that want to enter

Pizza!
fast janissaries challenge heavy artillery
for a delivery

look
the times of flags are not over
upon the banner slides the ethnic resin
men   and women
in uniform
awaken a drunk

Canári Uorf

...i ‘nalter dei sdilinqua
copin’alingua
de’ e clasi moar laki...

razzi’e al podér con confiúsd grimagne
in di lugares umbrusi ov Sciarlettaun
in i varaiti stori ov Micc Leik

‘i uét strittucarri no scelterano
i no dan jobba ‘n’un camin indre’
purtieri tignusi ti puscian a’lpurgatori

lassaieme tiatri andar di bridgis
lassaieme cu-anos in exail che
dan miusic end cruassanzz a tulemónd

talía/mira/lúk/

fa’ bala l’occ camu... ‘a ciucca de’indians sdilinqua
ormá’sc-iuppa’, inciudá da’ivertigin

‘a spussa de’icessi ciapa Quin strít
indi cornar unne u’strittucarru talia mutu

la laina ciciarona ov cildren of emigranzz
che vuogghion trasi’

pizza!
fast gianiserr pelean contra di evi artíglieri
for e deliveri

Vardé!
taims ov flegs ar not ovarr
in copp’ogonfalón sbava la resin etinica
omeni   i fimmini
co’adivisa
ueikáp i’lborracio

THEY ARE NOT ADMITTED INTO THE LAND OF LAKES THOSE EMBRACING THEIR OWN SHADOW drowned in a puddle of vomit the sidewalk drenched

SE PODE NO FURNIGA' CUNT A'SCIADO-U INDI TIERA OV LEIKSS
'fogada in'e puzzacchia ov vomit
di saiduolk uét

read

here in the charter of rights
there is no room for
infibulations, turbans, polygamy, sexual violence,
purges, smokers, only tomato in de bekiarda

in the world of errant farmers
they don't plant homosexuality
they till the earth

and they forgive only the animals

ríd,lieggi

Achí in di Ciartarovraitz
no ai lugar foar
fiche moncá',turbánt,becafiche,iulensa carnal,
purghe,smokars, onli tomato in'di bakiarda

ne'lmonno de'contadini vagabundd
no se planta 'afroceria
se fatica la tiera

i se perdona sultántt 'ibesti

the Chinese get on the streetcar
older than the temples of sweat
they don't ask for directions

or buy citizenships

towards the Communist temple
the Long Realty March
brings new invasions

barbarians

the mortgages rebound o€ the walls of the Reichmans
the fate of the
umane genti is shattered

i cines' ciargian u'strittucarru
veci piu' de'itempolls de'ssuét
i no addumánnan por info

i compran minga scitisenscíp

asta 'ltempoll comunist'
la longamarcia de'rrialesteitt
mena niú ciargiate

barbari

i giús crien su'l mur ovdi Raiccman
i morgheggi pusciati via sfasan
i'destin de'iuman pipoll

I return home inebriated from a wedding of the masses

respect ancestries
and blood

no more entwining   no lovers' quarrels
too many envelopes to count
who will show the sheets stained with blood...

on the balcony the geraniums shimmer
moist with musk
the old men watch blindly

Turnu a'cá ciúk foar a ueddin de'e masse

Rispect'di antenatt
end di blád

no moar infornade no moar menade d'amor
tumeni envelopps tu caunt
ú ll displeí'ilinzoli luordi d'eblád...

su'lbalcon i gerann ar sperlusenti
uét de'moscado
i veci talían i non

dear mother
they have put hounds in front of the gates
to defend villas, Palladio
lucky for him! is dead,
here they are all presidents, mother
the houses have more columns than the Parthenon
they erected a long wall that surrounds their homes
perhaps it is better like this

they have the cars of the Italian rich
but they make more noise

they have children that are proud of their italian origin
when they beat up a transvestite

mother we are in an Italy that is not of the north
nor of the center nor of the south
it isn't shaped like a boot
perhaps a patent leather shoe

mother I could tell you many things
but I must say goodbye

p.s. mother dear mother
    u' zappatore
    died
    yesterday
    of cirrhosis of the liver
    the organ wounded
    by wartime echoes of must

cara matri
anno mettuto dogs davann'igheitt
pe'addeffennere bildíng che 'lPaladio
fortunado elu! L'e' mort,
achí sun tuti presidénzz madar
le ause g'an moar colone del Partenun
dei bild una long uól araund eloro ause
peréps l'é mei inscí

Lur a ghan cars com'li aitaliann co'a grana
ma'son moar trabbolmeikar

Lur a ghan guaglioni che sún práud tu bí aitalian
cuanno tarellan'nnfemminiello

mama uí ar in 'na Itálí che l'e' no de'lnoff
ne' delsenter ne' del sutt
la gá no la forma de 'na bbút
meibi d'n sammer sciú

mama vi pudaria scriviri tant coss
ma Ai mast sei gudbai

p.s. mama cara mama
    u'zappatore
    l'e' mort
    aier
    de'ciross
    l'organn sgarrupato
    da'i memori di musti belicosi

Garbage for all seasons

the global village spreads the hundred odors of a thousand
foods cooked and not, according to custom
and the urban waste of a thousand races
each with its own little
green bag to forget
pluriracial factories of rheum sweat shit
multiculturalism for a thousand multidisposals
italojamaican indochinese
blackwhites yellowreds
canada all-inclusive+separatism and a trip to cuba
warm warmth violent cyclothymic
dio! come sa di sale lo pane altrui

Garbiccio for oll sison's

di glóbol villegg com'n pavún displeis 'a su roda di tausandz
odúr ov andrez'z fúd cúkd end nott laikk in di oldcauntri
i urban garbicci ov táusand'z razzi'e
ogne co'nla su'
littol bléc bega per desmentegar
fattorie multipipoll ov cispasuétscít
mult... foar tausandz ov multijettagarbiccio
aitalmaruchinindociainis
negheruaít gialorosi
canada ollincluded+separasión end e trip tu Kiúba
caliente calor iúlento arraggiato
Dio cum é salá'l pan de'i alter!

Open College

the bars of College street are opening
open Brooklyn
you of granita
and of espressos
tables on the sidewalks and children of immigratory waves

the Chinese State knocks noisily
"we will stop them on the waterline!"
from pool halls upstairs
appear young portuguese

night falls with a group of vietnamese
knifing each other
("sons of war" they say)
at night a gang of vigilantes
clean-shaven italoportojapokrainian
maybe chase a car thief

the yell in ENGLISH
poly, multi thugs

open College

they could close off the area
like in Rome
and put tables
in the streets!
the summer is different on College
and the distant sirens
belong to the city
on College bells are ringing
on College firetrucks are a civic event
on College they know you
on College there is a vagrant
that everyone knows
and that goes back and forth
along College

Collegg ciudad abierta

i'bbar ov Collegg strít openn
open Brúklin
ov granita
i ov expresss
teibolls ovar di saiduók end figghi de'unne immigratori

u'ciainis steitt noks bacanous
"Li stopperem ovar di bagnasciughi!"
from pulhol da'lprimeiro piso
iáng poltughiscc scio-u a'cara

la nott vegn co'na banda ov vietnamís
che se sbudéla
"figghi de'a ghera" dei sei
la nott e gheng ov vigilantes
sbarba' aitoloportogippokrainian
peréps ran pe'mená' 'nlader de'ccarru

gridajittanti 'n'inglés
multipicadores

open Collegg

pudarissen sara' 'l neiboár
conn in Romm
end put di teibollss
in di strítz !
sammar l'é diferente a Collegg
i le sirenn luntan
che vegnn da'acitá
lur ar not de'Collegg
a Collegg sonan le campán
a Collegg todoelmundo te canusce
a Collegg a lé un closciárd
un bombo che tuti canusce
e che v'avant'indré
pe'cCollegg

the pantograph of a streetcar
tears through the viscera of the sky
hunks of watermelon
bits of pistachio ice cream
scraps of tomato
and threads of parmesan and pecorino
rain
upon the tables of College

l'antinna d'u'strittucarru
derva lo stomago ov di skái
slaiss de uotarmelon
muzzicade de aiscrím al pistaci
sgagnate de tomáto
end fil de grana i pecorino
scravassa
ovar di teibolls ov Collegg

Italian Saturday

the area awakens to the sound
of AlfaRomeo and Cherokees
"It's Saturday"
a spring Saturday
we must air out the garages
"wake up Nina and put on your best dress!"
Tony will buy cannoli
while nonno hoes the bekiarda
to plant flowers and not tomatoes
like they taught him
(in adult education)

here in the Petawawa of the rich
of the less rich and of the neveragain poor
the sun shines italian

it's nice to see the cotrarelli
playing be-se-ból
in the streets
and the old men sitting on the steps near
the neoclassic garage

it's warm and the linen clothes are lying
on the bed still fragrant
double-breasted suits and flowered shirts from
Florida

the mothers and the nonnas are preparing cannelloni
the wine stirs in the cellars
waiting for relatives   friends
how nice it is to walk along the empty streets of
Woodbridge

knowing each other
after years in the neighborhood

Aitalian sabatu

di neiboar se despierta al son de'
Alfaromeo i Cirokiis
"Iz saciurdei "
saciurdai ov springg
lezz openn i garagis
"ueikáp Nina i mettute u'dress piu'beddu !"
Tony baï'icanoli
cuando il nono zappera' a'bbakiarda
pe'ppianta' i'flauar i not tomátos
come li ann ampara' in di scúl
ov di neiboar

achí ne la Petauaua de'chiddi co' idané
de' iless ricc i de'nevareghein bombi
'l sán sperlus'aitalian

Izz naiss mirar i cotrarelli
plei beseból
in di strítz
end i veci acchianá su'isteps
vicinu a'lgaragg niúclasic

Izz hott end i dressi de lin descansan
su'l'lett ancúr odorús
i dabbollbrestti i 'e camiss co'ffiuri de la
Floridá

matri end grenmaders cúk i'canelún
i vin arraggiati in di basamenti
ueitin' foar 'iparentt end l'amis
com'e' bell camina' pe'istrítz vacanti
ov Vúdbrígg

strusciarse
aftar iears ov laiff in di neiboarr

there are no cafes
there are no shops
the pools still dirty
the trees so young
there is shade only
near the neoclassic garages
there are no barbers
pharmacists
and the priest...

... it is an italian sun
that beats down on Woodbridge
flowered Woodbridge
one day they will put benches
for the old men
confined in their maximum security bekiardas

ghe' ne' minga de trani end pabb
ghe'ne' minga de stóri
di suimmin'púl ancuora lordi
larbuli ancuora iang
ghe'ne'minga de frescura
dumá vicinu a'iggaragg niúclasic
ghe'ne'minga de' barbé'
e de spesié
end el pret...

...l'é 'n aitalian sán
che pica ovar Vúdbrigg
Vúdbridgg 'nfiorada Vúdbridgg silensiusa
nu jiuornu uandei Dei putt i'bbence
per i veci
prisoneri ne'e bakiarde de masima sicuresa

THE TRANSLATED MESSAGES DON'T ARRIVE

not the thunderous cries of the last orator
nor the double-face flyers

we are ashamed of our ignorance
italia what is left of us? in us?

we have no clothing to wash in Don Mills and our
empire survives in the busts of il Duce
we will build other ghettos for our children and
the other races to come

after us Ceramicaland
Woodbridge on the lake
Morgheggioville...
here where the highways
lead to the italian enclave
the messages brought by the last orator
don't arrive

"We have built it all and now we own it..."
in the summer old men resemble street signs
in the still Italian corridors

NON ARRIVANO I MESSAGGI TRADOTTI

no 'iscrím bacaiun de'lultim politicari
no i'vvolantin dublefass

uí ar esceimd pe'a nostr'gnuransa
italí 'uozz left de num ? in num ?

notenemos ropa da lava' in di don mills
i el'nost imperio vive ancuora ne' imediocuerpos de'lduce
uill bild moar ghetos pe'nnostri figghi i
li adar razzi'e che vegnarán.

Aftar ás Ceramicalend,
Vudbrigg on di leikk,
Morgheggiovill...
Achí donde las careteras
bring tú di aitalian steitt,
Achí no'arivan di messagis
de'ultimm politicari.

" Iú evv biltt Trónto end adess l'é vostra...."
d'estatt i veci son comm'isaina
ne'iquiett aitalian corridors

Paradise of citizenship

I am horny for the community's triumph
I inhale global villages
sub tegmine fagi
I titillate multicultural clitorises

Expo
god
if you are in your heaven
if you don't have a colour
a language
a tribal mask
an Alinari photo
show me the paradise of citizenship
should I tell you who I am?

I don't want to die here
because my pride of fatherland
is boundless
insatiable like my appetite
not mediterranean but prehistoric
I'm Rossi's coffee pot, towered, babelic
I'm an angel in underwear by Chia
and I'm an angel in brocade by Beato Angelico
I'm as desolate as a factory by Sironi
I'm the premature brother of Rocco
the brick and the pick of the Wall
I'm confined for the short time of a life
I'm a chameleon of ethnicity
but not a merchant
I'm the helmsman who falls asleep

Expo
god
unveil to me the paradise of citizenship

Paradais

Me gozo ‘l trionff comunitari
smello ‘aspussa ov di globol villegis
subtegminefagi
titillo multichiulciurál bernarde

Expo
Dio
se ti te se’
si no tiene un colór
‘nalingua
‘n’antik mascara
‘na picciar de’iAlinar
derve i paradaiss ov scitisenscip
Chi sun? Sciuddaitelliu?

nochieromorirachí
bicaus ‘l mí praidd de patria
no gá fronteras
‘l ga’ semperr famm
no mediteranei bat prestorico
Iju sugnu ‘namoka de’lRossi,smerlada,incasinada
Iju sugnu ‘nangiul in culottz de’lChia end
‘n’angiul i’nbrocad de’lBeatiAngelici
sugnu desola’ comm ‘nafactori de’lSironi
sugnu ‘l fradel setimin de’lRocco
dibríkenddipík ov di uól
in esili por ‘nratito ov mai laiff
Iju sugnu ‘ncamaleonti etinico bat
no soi ‘nmercantt
Aiém ‘ldraivér ú folls eslíp

Expo
Signur
open i’pparadais ov scitisenscip tu mí!

Honest Ed's

didn't you see them?   the races
sucking their teeth
spitting on subway platforms
throwing a hundred pounds of meat on the barbecue
buying tons of sugar
for fear of war
going into big stores
bait of voracious sects

dreaming of wardrobes with mirrored doors
buying bread and bread
stowing supermarket bags in the trunks of
american cars
buying gold and gold

sleeping in immigration offices
queued to go to unknown factories
in the suburbs of your sight
unloaded by a bus
on a Sunday

discounts
on leg of lamb
in line at the food-banks
in lines faint, drowsy, feverish

can't you see the fear of poverty
the steps of a second life
slippery from sweat?

sleeping little and always being sleepy
the brain wearied
from di€erent languages

there are weddings
already marked by the violence of broken dreams

Onestéz

Nun li vidisti i'razzi'e ?
sakiare i'dinti cu'ffischi de frontera
lanzando scaracchi su' banchi ov di sábuei
jettare e andred punti ov mit su'lbbarbecchiú
cumpra' tanzss ov sciugár
por scaggia de la ghera
ciargiari di cardz in da storo

rent the closezz co'i' anti uid mirrar
cumpra' pan y pan
fill co'nsupermarket beghe el maletéro
ov americancars
cumpra' gold & gold

durmi' in de immigrescion offis
in la láina ne' sabarbs de'a tu'ociada
jettati co'l paracadu' in annón factoris
lodati da un trocco
dominical

discaunz
en cuoscia de agneddu
in la láina alle fudbencs
in le láina smort, amodorradas,ca'fievre

e cu' non vitte a' paura ov poverti
di stepsss ov e second laiff'
scarlighent foar suét ?

durmi'...poco i siempre indurmentá'
lu' breinn straccu pe'
lingui d'atro monno

ci stan ueddíngs ia' marcade
da la viulensa ov brochen dríms

you so young
will lose your ethnic shape

will become fat and pakistani
you a varicose portuguese

your children will play be-se-ból
the turkish grandmother will watch football games on television

you will build a fence around
your italian meatball
and put a sign on it
"PLEASE DON'T REMIND ME OF THE PAST"

iu' so iang
t'impanzerai etnicamente

'daddiventare fat i paki
end iu' poltughiscc coi veni autdóar

i vostri cotrári plei a'beseból
a'madre turca taliera' u' futbóll
a la tiví

iu' bilderá''nafensa
araund iúr aitalian mitboll
cunt saina
"PLIAS NUN'ME RICURDA' U'PASSA'..."

The Murder of Bossi

you looked at me with vacuous eyes
when I spoke of Gramsci
you asked me
if this italy was a civilized country

you will find three lines at customs
one for the european community
one for the rest of the world
and one for i terroni

fate la nanna coscine di pollo
sweet italocanadian spy
mentre la nonna cucina il cavallo
from the south to the north in less than a month
sotto il ponte di Baracca
you left to kill Bossi
c'é Pierin che fa la cacca
you are not afraid of hills and streams

'l killing de'lBossi

mi taliavi co'li occ astutati
cuanno Ai tolkd de 'lGramsci
mi preguntavi
si cchista Italí l'era un país civíl

Ti te buscará tri laina a l'aduana
vuna por 'a comunidá iuropían
vuna for di resto o'munno
i vuna per i terón

fate la nanna coscine di pollo
suít spai terorista italocanadés
mentre la nonna cucina il cavallo
dal sutt al noff in less de 'n més
sotto il ponte di baracca
Iú partisti tu kill 'lBos(s)i
c'e' pierin che fa' la cacca
ti no g'a paura de'fiumm e'dos(s)i

Baggio, Rozzano, Quarto Oggiaro
it isn't easy
to recognize the old ghettos
from the new... and Giambellino

children of Europe
that do not run
faster than Miglio

darknesses distant and heavy
Bari or Toronto
the young play
and copulate
kneeling before the Samnites

Bagio,Rosán,Quartogiaro
l'e' minga facil
recognaizz i veci negher
da chiddi novi...et Giambelino

figghi d'Iúrópa
che no'ran
fastar de 'u'nMiglio

Bui luntán i chiatti pereps sin taimm
bari o trónto
i'cotrari si scialan
i fornigan
forchi de'ltemp sanita

the fog has covered the countryside
nature is on all fours
sodomized it whispers
"at your disposal"

the farmers still talk to the animals
the races, colours speak of values
"more justice is needed"

ex-nations ask for money
from happy states
the fog asks for kickbacks
blood is seen and not seen

you imagine that the countryside was here
but do you see it?

la niegghia ‘l ga’cuerto u’campu
la natura si mete a’la pecurina
trombata sospira
“ad’disposizione”

i vilan parlan ancuora con’ianimalia
di razzi’end li colors parlan de’ valur
ghe voll moar giástiss

ex nescion preguntan foar mani
a’l’eppi néscion
la niegghia chiere u’pizzu
u’blád se’talia i non se’talia

se fantastica che achí era ‘a campagna
ma ti te ghe vedi ?

in the shadow of the monument to the injured worker
artists ambulate
they talk about everything

of cousins that arrived empty-handed
of funerals that cost too much
of italians that have abandoned their homes

of basamenti to rebuild
of whorish daughters
of property tax

you have left to kill Bossi
without knowing who Gramsci is
you don't know what it means to rest
in the shade of a Party

weakened by sweet domestic violence
you have left without permission
in the name of honour
indi€erent to the banners
of Petawawa
to the calls of the sirens
emerging from the oceans of Woodbridge
sickened by the plankton
of malls

I wish for you the bench of infinity

Sut'alombra de'lmonumentu al'ingiurd uorkar
struscian 'li artisti
se abla de todo

de'icusinn che 'lgan minga pagá u'pleitt
de' funeral checcost tu macc
de'iaitalians che an lassa' la mogliera

de'basamenti tu renoveit
de'e figghie slandre
de'properti taxx

iú ev left tu kill i'lBossi
sin saver chi l'e' 'l Gramsci
iú donnou ciccós mins descansar
n'suta l'ombra del partido

sdilinqua'por 'na suítt iulensa in l'ausa
Iú partisti uivaut pirmissu
per u'ndelittu donori
ti te ne freghi de'eflegs
ov Petauaua
de'e canson de'esirén
ch'esusan da'ioceani ov Vúdbrigg
schifata da'lplanton
de' molls

vogghio pa'ttia 'abencia de'linfinido

Cinematic Taxi

a taxi of an ex-colonel of the
afghan army or a
somali refugee
or perhaps of a milanese survivor
travels the streets without time
and without memory

Toronto
the streets are empty even when
there are people

avenues
lashed by wind
journeys of solitary titans

it's not a city for lovers   Toronto
the streets are long and wide
the buildings severe
the complicitous doorways are in Milan

you too little girl torn away
by ethnic cleansing
for your personal hygiene
toast with a jamaican taxi driver
just stopped by the police

toast for shitizenship
wanted
desired
fornicated
defecated
and then swallowed again

taxi driver
let's sing the national anthem
to the sound of the meter

Cinima in Tassí

nu chéb de'nex colonél
de'armada afganistana
o de'n refugius maruchín
o pereps de'nsorvaivor milanés
vá pe'istrítz uidáut taimm
i memori

Trónto
di strítz de'ciel pienn de nuvuli
afama' de gentt

aveniú
mazziá da'uvientu
traversa' da titan soligni

l'é no citá por lávers Trónto
'i strítz son long end largg
di stiff bildíngs
i purtún filoss ar 'n Milán

anca ti putela scippata
da'a pulisia etinica
foar a class de igien vital
trinca cunt'ntasista giameican
stoppato da'a polisia

tost per dis cittamerdanza
voluda
desiderada
infornada
cagada
i po'ingoiada

tasista
lezzsin di nescional andem
a'lsaundde'ltasameter

Multicultural Christmas

the buildings in Comasina echo
from petit bourgeois christmases
to the roots of condominiums
kinetic junkies

in the spirals of housing projects
jamaican progeny
develop in darkness

italians clean fish
cries of a hundred babies
and neighborhoods in a frenzy

exhalations of incense
vomiting of curry and parked taxis
faint but strong-willed
a song makes its way
to my room

amore love amor
we are all immigrants
you are not excluded either
diaphanous jew
alone and without ideology
persecuted for a hundred years by the Bolsheviks

you will be there too cuban engineer
bonus in a tourist package
(walking one day with a flag)
toward the Skydome

no one is absent from the roll-call of races,
of origins, of creed
it is the christmas of the Charter of Rights
disloyal Lolita toast to your
arrogance
fondled by suburban DJ's

Crísmás multicruturál

di Comasina bildíng's risaund
ov Crísmás sufega'
ai rúzz de' bildíngs
tosici agita'

ne'irings de'iprojects
il midolo giameicán
crisci ne'ldarkk

di aitalians clín di fiscc
scríms ov andredz putei
i barrios in deliri

odúr de'ncensi
vomitade di cárri
chebs parcati end snorin'
legera ma sin scantu atraca una cansión
fin a'a mi rúm

amore amor ammuri
Uí ar óll immigranz
nianca tí te se'fora
sdilinquata Giú
sola i sin ideolohía
sgarrupata per undredz iears da'bolsevikk

Iú'll bi aiá ingegner cu-ána
bonus ov e tiuristic packegg
uán dei in camin
astal'ostadio

nisciuno falta a'laciamada de'razzi'e,
de'e origin,de'e confesión
lé 'lCrismás de'a Ciartovraitz trinca il vin matura' ne'ldarkk
de cantin vecie (boccalun!)nevar fermenta' in di basamenti
tignusa Lolita trinca a'a tu''rogansa
filada daddigeis de'borgada

you too are set in jewelry
... you too radiant princess
without jewels and without a land
infatuated with the last multicultural hybrid

and you that once
were a whore of the lebanese
and perhaps could confer upon yourself the title

of pearl of the West

today you have a son and a husband
from the third world
a Harvard graduate

a polyglot son
who does not take candies from strangers
and will die of aids

only because there are no more revolutions
you do not have to spend winters
in the bosom of your mother
you
will return
like all the thousands
the hundreds of thousands
of chinese, latin american,
from ex-nations
from ex-states

maybe there will no longer be gigantic waves
inevitably
pulled by the undertow
onto these beaches

it is a snowstorm that is coming
we will learn

anca ti bela piedra per 'lgiuél
...anca ti bela prinsesa
sin giuéls i sin tiera
inamorada ov di last 'sperimentu multicrutural

i anca ti che taimm egó
l'eri 'aslandra de'libanés
i pereps te ciamavi

perla de'luestt

túdei ti te gá 'un puteo i 'un maridi
co'alaura
d'Árruard

n'figghiu che poliglotico
ciapa minga caremele da'lpedichiurr
i morera' sin duda ov éidzz

sol picché no'ncistannu mas rivolusión
ti te ghe no de migra'
tra'i zinne de'a madar
Ti
te vegnaré 'ndré
comm tutt 'itausandz
di undred tausandz
de' cines,sudamerican,
da ex cauntris
da'iexsteitt

pereps no'saran mas i cavalún
sin duda
pusciati da'a risaca
ovar dis bicis

l'e' 'na tempesta de neff che ariva
Nu imparerόm

to show our most beautiful colours
multi-coloured balls
for the christmas tree

a'displei auar most biútifúl colors
bale multicolorade
foar di crísmás trii

Eboli

awakened from the American dream
when on the prairies
public housing is being erected
stifling the view

Rome and Kensington market
burn
but no one knows

hosts of seagulls
fly on the rotten plain
distant smells shatter
against the doors of neoclassic garages

the air-conditioners are useless
against the fumes
of Caribana

hypothesizing in the streets
the tanks of Pinochet
and of Krushev
are parked at the borders

portuguese italians somalis palestinians

the ethnics

work in agencies for cleansing

algid garbage mutates
like a stone smoothed
and inevitably crushed
by the undertow

the windows
of Yonge Street shatter
beneath the pressure of exuberant hydrants

Eboli

S'arrueglia da' l americhendrimm
quanno ne'e preiris
s'azan l'ausi populár
che súfegán l'uciada

Romm i'l mercá'd'iKensintón
brusan
bát nisun sa

armi de sigulls
svolasan su'apiana incrostada
tanfa rimott crascis
contr'iclerr de'igaragis niuclasic

inutile l'e' l'ercondiscionin'
contra 'lvapuri
de'lCaribana

in di strítz se fantastica
i tanki de'lPinoscét
i de'lCrusciόv
'stan parcati a'a frontera

poltughiscc, aitalians, marucchí', palestiness

i razzi'e

fatican in compagnie de'pulisia etinica

smort garbicci icambian
com'a piedra levigada
end sind duda pusciati
d'arisaca

di uindos ov Iang strít
se fracasan
sut'apresión di imbriaghe pompp

clitorises are mutilated
death penalties in parking lots
t-shirts soaked with beer
in front of monotonous televisions
hyperventilated populations
watch from porches
mute and nostalgic

generations without remote control
sweat profusely
at the shows
of democracy

filthy!
where Socrates' pædophilia is punished
by millennia
hemlock and castor oil
for the ghosts of High Park

mixed couples
pornoanglophone triangles
respectful and calvinistic families
they don't leave a tip
on the tables
of the latest italian restaurant

Toronto
I want to smoke a cigarette
I want to become a cigarette
the smoke for a hundred thousand allergy su€erers
I am the Masaniello of the smoking section
I want to fly onto plates of eggplant and zucchini
to mix myself into the fierce curries
to roll myself in a fajita
like boric acid fumarole to stir rice and chicken
to ride the draft of an air conditioner
to camouflage myself in the hundred year old dust of
carpeting

se tagghian 'ebernarde
'masamenti'n di parchinglott
canotte suétt de'bira
infrontov tiví cunanti
pipol sufega'
talian da' pisi astutati
end oldcauntrorosi

generescion uivaút rimotcontroll
suét laikk pigs
a'isciovs
de'a democrasia

sgarrupati vuatri
donde 'afroceria de' lSocratis l'e' castigada
from tausandz iears
velen i oli de ricin
ppe'ifantasimi de Haihparc

capolls misc-iade,
triangul pornoanglofonici,
familí per ben i calvinistici
Lur lassan minga la mancia
on di teibolss
de'l'ultim aitalian restauránt

Trónto
Mi vojo smokk 'na sigarétt
Aiuontt addiventá 'na sicarietta
il smokk foar andredz sufegá
Aiém 'l Masaniell ovdismokin'dipartment
i vurria vula' su' ppiatti di melanciana e zuchino,
furnigá' co'icarri arraggiati,
fa' icaprioll in'a faíta,
com'nmulinell mis-ciar i cichen
cummattiri 'larie de 'n eircondiscioner
camaleontarme ne'a fufa centenari
d'emochetts

to trans-humanize with the pots in Chinatown
like a poisonous gust of wind to sti€en the backs
of a thousand baby-kissing politicians
I would be the bad breath of repentant DJ's
the chloroses of the running multitudes
the fetid and caustic membrane
of shining skyscrapers

fly with me
toward the last recesses of a health conscious democracy
permeate the pulmonary basements
of this city that doesn't know how to scream
like a Harpy
I would like to sprinkle amber
on the beaches
of our solitude

svapora' da'i marmitt ov Ciainataun
spacá 'esc-iene com'nventicello velenosso
ov tausandz politicari chissingbabis
vurria ca fussi l'alito tanfuss de'digeispentirosi
'a tibicí ov pipoll de cursa
la skinn fetusa i sbrusante
de gratacieli sperlusenti

flai cummia
asta 'i ultimm ammucciamenti de'a democrasia salutosa
isparpagliati ne'basamenti de'pulmonn
de'stacitá che sa minga vusá
com'arpia
vurria jettá' merda
ovar di bicis
de' e noster solignitá

Corrado Paina lives and writes in Toronto. He is published in Canada by Mansfield Press: Hoarse Legend (2000), The Dowry of Education (2004), The Alphabet of the Traveler (2006), and Souls in Plain Clothes (2008). He was the editor of College Street — Little Italy Toronto's Renaissance Strip, a finalist for the Toronto Heritage Award. In Italy he has published a collection of short stories entitled di corsa (Monteleone/Mapograph — Vibo Valentia), the novel tra Rothko e tre finestre (Ibiskos), the collections of poetry tempo rubato (Atelier 14 — Milano) darsena inquinata (Moderata durant — Latina), l'alfabeto del viaggiatore (Silvio Editrice) and Abecedario (with etchings by Sandro Martini, printed by Paolo Nava).

Other Books From Mansfield Press

Poetry

Leanne Averbach, *Fever*
Nelson Ball, *In This Thin Rain*
Nelson Ball, *Some Mornings*
Gary Barwin, *Moon Baboon Canoe*
George Bowering, *Teeth: Poems 2006–2011*
Stephen Brockwell, *Complete Surprising Fragments of Improbable Books*
Stephen Brockwell & Stuart Ross, eds., *Rogue Stimulus: The Stephen Harper Holiday Anthology for a Prorogued Parliament*
Diana Fitzgerald Bryden, *Learning Russian*
Alice Burdick, *Flutter*
Alice Burdick, *Holler*
Jason Camlot, *What The World Said*
Margaret Christakos, *wipe.under.a.love*
Pino Coluccio, *First Comes Love*
Marie-Ève Comtois, *My Planet of Kites*
Dani Couture, *YAW*
Gary Michael Dault, *The Milk of Birds*
Frank Davey, *Poems Suitable for Current Material Conditions*
Pier Giorgio Di Cicco, *The Dark Time of Angels*
Pier Giorgio Di Cicco, *Dead Men of the Fifties*
Pier Giorgio Di Cicco, *The Honeymoon Wilderness*
Pier Giorgio Di Cicco, *Living in Paradise*
Pier Giorgio Di Cicco, *Early Works*
Pier Giorgio Di Cicco, *The Visible World*
Salvatore Difalco, *What Happens at Canals*
Christopher Doda, *Aesthetics Lesson*
Christopher Doda, *Among Ruins*
Glenn Downie, *Monkey Soap*
Rishma Dunlop, *The Body of My Garden*
Rishma Dunlop, *Lover Through Departure: New and Selected Poems*
Rishma Dunlop, *Metropolis*
Rishma Dunlop & Priscila Uppal, eds., *Red Silk: An Anthology of South Asian Women Poets*
Ollivier Dyens, *The Profane Earth*
Laura Farina, *Some Talk of Being Human*
Jaime Forsythe, *Sympathy Loophole*
Carole Glasser Langille, *Late in a Slow Time*
Suzanne Hancock, *Another Name for Bridge*
Jason Heroux, *Emergency Hallelujah*
Jason Heroux, *Memoirs of an Alias*
Jason Heroux, *Natural Capital*
John B. Lee, *In the Terrible Weather of Guns*
Jeanette Lynes, *The Aging Cheerleader's Alphabet*
David W. McFadden, *Be Calm, Honey*
David W. McFadden, *Shouting Your Name Down the Well: Tankas and Haiku*
David W. McFadden, *What's the Score?*
Leigh Nash, *Goodbye, Ukulele*
Lillian Necakov, *The Bone Broker*
Lillian Necakov, *Hooligans*
Peter Norman, *At the Gates of the Theme Park*
Peter Norman, *Water Damage*
Natasha Nuhanovic, *Stray Dog Embassy*
Catherine Owen & Joe Rosenblatt, with Karen Moe, *Dog*
Corrado Paina, *The Alphabet of the Traveler*
Corrado Paina, *The Dowry of Education*
Corrado Paina, *Hoarse Legend*
Corrado Paina, *Souls in Plain Clothes*
Stuart Ross et al., *Our Days in Vaudeville*
Matt Santateresa, *A Beggar's Loom*
Matt Santateresa, *Icarus Redux*
Ann Shin, *The Last Thing Standing*
Jim Smith, *Back Off, Assassin! New and Selected Poems*
Jim Smith, *Happy Birthday, Nicanor Parra*
Robert Earl Stewart, *Campfire Radio Rhapsody*
Robert Earl Stewart, *Something Burned on the Southern Border*
Carey Toane, *The Crystal Palace*
Priscila Uppal, *Summer Sport: Poems*
Priscila Uppal, *Winter Sport: Poems*
Steve Venright, *Floors of Enduring Beauty*
Brian Wickers, *Stations of the Lost*

Fiction

Marianne Apostolides, *The Lucky Child*
Sarah Dearing, *The Art of Sufficient Conclusions*
Denis De Klerck, ed., *Particle & Wave: A Mansfield Omnibus of Electro-Magnetic Fiction*
Paula Eisenstein, *Flip Turn*
Sara Heinonen, *Dear Leaves, I Miss You All*
Marko Sijan, *Mongrel*
Tom Walmsley, *Dog Eat Rat*

Non-Fiction

George Bowering, *How I Wrote Certain of My Books*
Rosanna Caira & Tony Aspler, *Buon Appetito Toronto*
Denis De Klerck & Corrado Paina, eds., *College Street–Little Italy: Toronto's Renaissance Strip*
Pier Giorgio Di Cicco, *Municipal Mind: Manifestos for the Creative City*
Amy Lavender Harris, *Imagining Toronto*
David W. McFadden, *Mother Died Last Summer*

To order these books, visit www.mansfieldpress.net